The Big Green Poetry Machine

Verses From The UK

Edited by Vivien Linton

First published in Great Britain in 2009 by:

 Young**Writers**

Young Writers
Remus House
Coltsfoot Drive
Peterborough
PE2 9JX
Telephone: 01733 890066
Website: www.youngwriters.co.uk

Foreword

Young Writers' Big Green Poetry Machine is a showcase for our nation's most brilliant young poets to share their thoughts, hopes and fears for the planet they call home.

Young Writers was established in 1991 to nurture creativity in our children and young adults, to give them an interest in poetry and an outlet to express themselves. Seeing their work in print will encourage them to keep writing as they grow, and become our poets of tomorrow.

Selecting the poems has been challenging and immensely rewarding. The effort and imagination invested by these young writers makes their poems a pleasure to enjoy reading time and time again.

Contents

St Richard's Catholic Primary School, Skelmersdale

Sharples CP School, Bolton

Tregoze Primary School, Swindon

West Walker Primary School, Newcastle Upon Tyne

Wimboldsley Primary School, Middlewich

The Poems

Make The World A Better Place

People of the world beware!
Before you start pulling out your hair.
It's as easy as can be,
So take a step and follow me!

The first thing to do is . . .
Pick up all the litter,
Come on, don't be bitter.
Let the world glitter!

The streets will shine,
But that is not all you can do.
I will take you all the way through;
Together we can help, me and you!

Next is recycling;
We all know it's true!
From bottles to stone,
We must not moan!

Paints and paper are good,
Copper wire and wood.
Finally, the solution to pollution . . .
Is walk or ride your bike.

Don't wait for it to get worse!
The ozone is about to burst.
This is such a terrible thing,
So stop and make the world sing.

Do all this, make yourself proud.
Put a smile on everyone's face!
Make the world a better place.

Lauren Cookson (9)
Ashbury Primary School, Swindon

What Lives In The World?

Beautiful butterflies,
Blind bats,
Buzzing bees.

Slow snails,
Slithering snakes,
Slimy slugs.

Wiggly worms,
Whizzing wasps,
Wailing wombats.

Dozy donkeys,
Dancing dogs,
Dizzy dragonflies.

Rodent rats,
Rude rabbits,
Roaring rhinos.

Gentle giraffes,
Giggling guinea pigs,
Generous gorillas.

Proud peacocks,
Pretty parrots,
Perfect penguins.

Lovely leopards,
Loving lions,
Little lizards.

What a wonderful world we live in.
Please take care of our world.

Sophie Charles (10)
Ashbury Primary School, Swindon

Save Our Planet

Our world is being hit by pollution,
Cars, factories, different vehicles, the cause of it all,
So we have to find a solution.

Try to use our cars less,
And do lots more walking,
So put an extra jumper over your dress,
Instead of turning up the heating.

When you plan your next holiday and think of flying,
Help the poor fish and polar bears who are dying.
It's our world out there,
So use some effort and try and stop this,
It's our environment we are saving!

Ella Griffiths (10)
Ashbury Primary School, Swindon

What A Wonderful World We Live In!

We live in a wonderful world that we see a lot of the time.
We like it, we care about it and most of all we treasure it.
We think of it as God because we care about Him too.
The world we live in has lots of animals that provide us
with food and drink.
Who made the animals?
God did so his people could live, work and feed their families.
We think if people trash our world, then we will not be happy.
Most of all we think of the world as a potato, because a potato is
hidden treasure.
So say thank you for our world!

Emma Louise Parker (8)
Ashbury Primary School, Swindon

What A Wonder-filled World!

War, war, what are you for?
Flash a smile and it's peace galore!

Disease, disease, cure with ease!
Not in poor countries, raise money please!

Recycle, recycle clothes and litter!
Or put rubbish in the bin,
It doesn't take any glamour or glitter!

We live in a word that is filled with pollution,
Please help us thrive and find a solution!

Millie Channon (9)
Ashbury Primary School, Swindon

The Rainforest

R is for rabbits, the cute fluffy things,
A is for apes that climb high in the trees,
I is for insects that crawl everywhere,
N is for night-time when stars shine so bright.
F is for fish that swim in the rivers,
O is for oranges, the fruit in the trees,
R is for rain to help all things grow,
E is for eggs when animals breed,
S is for sunshine to keep all things warm,
T is for tigers to scare predators away.

Anabelle Ruggiero (9)
Ashbury Primary School, Swindon

My Thoughts On Litter

When I see litter, it makes me angry from side to side,
It is unnecessary whether you're tall, small, thin or wide.
Kicking it around is silly and lazy as I know,
The smell is stinky and I just want to yell, 'No!'
The sight is dreadfully messy and that is something we all know.
If everybody helps we can really make a difference,
If we all have some confidence.
No matter who we are, we all live on Earth,
So let's show some respect for our own bit of turf.

Francesca Jenkins (10)
Ashbury Primary School, Swindon

Litter, Litter, It Should Go

Litter
Litter
Scoop it up
Litter
Litter
Before you chuck

Litter
Litter
It makes you frown
Litter
Litter
It pollutes your town

Litter
Litter
You should know
Litter
Litter
That it should go!

Declan McGann (11)
Cheadle Heath Primary School, Stockport

Litter

Litter,
Litter,
On the floor.
Litter,
Litter,
We don't want anymore!

Litter,
Litter,
All over the place.
Litter,
Litter,
There's no clean space!

Litter,
Litter,
I want it to go!
But,
Litter,
Litter,
Is going very slow.

Litter,
Litter,
Take it on your chin,
Litter,
Litter,
Put it in the bin!

Thomas Fahy (10)
Cheadle Heath Primary School, Stockport

At War

There are people in the world today
At war,
Risking their lives,
More and more.

This makes me so incensed, outraged, so mad,
I feel so helpless, despondent, so sad.

There are people in the world today,
At war,
Dying for nothing,
How much more?

This makes me feel so incensed, outraged, so mad,
I feel so helpless, despondent, so sad.

Why can't we all be friends
And look out for one another?
There's no need for war,
Our world can be fighting no more.

If we all put down our arms,
And choose armistice instead of war,
There will be no more torture,
We will have peace for evermore!

Chelsea McEvoy (11)
Cheadle Heath Primary School, Stockport

Help!

Our world is not a nice place
With everything out of order.

Help by turning off your water
Recycling things too.

Help by walking places rather than driving,
So the world can be saved!

Alexandra Spratt (10)
Cheadle Heath Primary School, Stockport

Poverty

Lying alone on a concrete floor,
Staring and staring at the sweet shop door.
Wishing and wishing for a house to own,
Can't even manage to get a loan.
Guess who?

Plodding along on the desert sand,
Travelling on across the land,
Reaching home with the water, hip, hip hooray!
I have walking a thousand miles today.
Guess who?

Today is the day my belly burst,
Now I am dying with thirst.
I am alive for now but I fear it won't last,
And very soon I'll be the past.
Guess who?

Enough of this death, destruction and war,
Now's the time to show poverty the door.
Recycle your junk and soon we will be,
The biggest and best happy family.
The person who wants change!

Bethany Cragg (10)
Cheadle Heath Primary School, Stockport

Stop!

Stop!
Don't kill the crocodiles.
You will miss them
When they are gone.
You kill them
Because of your shoes
Or for your bag!

Aron Erdelyi (10)
Cheadle Heath Primary School, Stockport

8

Litter, Litter, All So Bitter!

Litter,
Litter,
Put it in the bin.

Litter,
Litter,
It will get caught in a fish's fin.

Litter,
Litter,
Don't put it on the floor.
Litter,
Litter,
Recycle it and get more.

Litter,
Litter,
It does a lot of harm.

Litter,
Litter,
Pick it up
And people will be calm.

Elliot McClean (10)
Cheadle Heath Primary School, Stockport

War Is Useless

War is bad.
War is mad.
War will always make you sad.
People are dying.
People are crying.
People are suffering.
The world should be peaceful.
The world should be calm and quiet.

Charlotte Daley (11)
Cheadle Heath Primary School, Stockport

Changing The World

The world is changing day by day,
While all the caring goes away,
The animals seem to disappear,
While we discard rubbish there and here.

The world is changing day by day,
But no one has anything positive to say,
The cars all breathe out vivid petrol fumes,
While our world is filled with gloom.

The world is changing day by day,
Global warming means it's cold in the middle of May,
But we can make it a better place,
If we put on a happy face.

The world is changing day by day,
But we can help in a million ways.
Some are reusing, reducing and recycling,
So come on, let those light bulbs go *ping!*

Jessica Lund (10)
Cheadle Heath Primary School, Stockport

Changing The World

Litter, litter, pick it up,
All day long you'll have good luck.
Reuse, recycle, do it now.
Save the trees from the row.
Babies crying, people dying.
Soldiers fighting.
Now the time has come to be smart
And help us all survive.
Pass your message onto your friend
And your luck will never end.

Kieran Carrington (11)
Cheadle Heath Primary School, Stockport

Litter, Litter

Litter
Litter
On the floor
Litter
Litter
On the seashore
Litter
Litter
Pick it up
Litter
Litter
Before you extinct a duck
Litter . . .
Litter . . .
Litter . . .
Litter.

Tommy Swales (11)
Cheadle Heath Primary School, Stockport

Life Is Too Short

People die day by day,
Our lives are saved, theirs are destroyed,
Life is too short to fight,
Mums and dads never say goodbye,
Let's live our lives in peace,
Because we are in fear of our enemies.
We can put a stop to this,
We can all be friends,
And stick together as one team,
That way no one dies,
And there will be no loss for loved ones,
Because life is too short.

Megan Williams (10)
Cheadle Heath Primary School, Stockport

Litter, Litter

There are bugs on beaches
And rats on roaches.
Litter, litter,
Pick it up.

What about the animals
Living on the coast?
Their lives are wasting
And it's our fault most.

Litter, litter,
Pick it up.

The pollution is gruesome
And it's killing the planet.

Erin Cosgrove (10)
Cheadle Heath Primary School, Stockport

Waste!

Our world is full of litter,
It is not a pleasant place to be,
The litter is simply appalling to see.

Don't waste water or food,
It will put Mother Nature in a bad mood,
There are people starving everywhere,
Don't waste food, have a care!
You can make a difference, have a say,
Cut down on waste, do it today.

Amy Buchan (10)
Cheadle Heath Primary School, Stockport

Litter

Litter, it's everywhere
There's even a rotten pear

Litter, it's been washed up by the sea
Please help me

Litter is very bad
It makes me very sad

Litter gets stuck to fishes' fins
So pick it up and put it in the bins.

Callum Mann (10)
Cheadle Heath Primary School, Stockport

World War II

World War II
We hate you,
Fighting is bad,
So now I'm sad.

We've got to stop the war,
And we'll make it a law,
Now we've made our amends,
We can all be friends.

Joshua Loftus (10)
Cheadle Heath Primary School, Stockport

Litter

I don't like litter, it is bad,
The streets look messy and scruffy,
It's not good to litter,
It is sad!

Jennifer Walsh (11)
Cheadle Heath Primary School, Stockport

Help Our World Please!

Our world is being destroyed by people chopping down our trees,
Which are our animals' habitats,
That people don't care about, please stop.
Don't destroy our world!

People need to stop using water when not needed.
Please stop global warming and help the animals.

The world that we live in can be helped, so do it.

Hazel Killingbeck (10)
Cheadle Heath Primary School, Stockport

Untitled

We don't want suffering,
We don't need killing,
We don't need war,
We don't need fighting,
We don't accept war.
So join hands
And make peace.

Adam Kennedy (10)
Cheadle Heath Primary School, Stockport

Think About It!

Think about rainforests, animals and extinction.
Think about war, disease and pollution.
Think about the homeless, the poor and unfortunate.
Care about the dying, injured and hurt.
Care about animals, plants and wildlife.
Care for the
             World!

Juliet Kearsey (9)
Colwall CE Primary School, Malvern

Save The World

Save the world,
Do your part
Or else the world will fall apart.

Animal extinction, take them away
Then in the future you'll have to pay.

Climate change, it's melting the ice,
Keep doing this and you'll pay the price.

Litter, pick up the clutter
Or else you'll be a litterbug nutter.

Pollution, use less of your car,
This little step will get you far.

Rainforests being cut down,
Make a protest, tell Gordon Brown.

Recycle card and plastic
To make the situation much less drastic.

You've saved the world,
You've done your part
And now the world won't fall apart.

Kate Barber (10)
Colwall CE Primary School, Malvern

We Need To Look After Them

Do you like animals? I do,
Especially endangered ones like the kakapo.
You might think that tigers are horribly scary,
Or the yak is just big and hairy,
But did you know an interesting fact?
Human beings are having an impact on these beautiful animals -
We're not looking after them!

Do you like the rainforests? I do,
But in the rainforests the animals are making a hullabaloo.
It's their habitat you see,
But we're cutting it down tree by tree and
We're not looking after them!

So let's sort this out.
Let's not cheat on a cheetah.
We don't want a Devil's Hole pupfish
To be a very fed up fish.
Let's say, 'aye-aye' to our animals and
Look after them!

Joshua Peter Lee (8)
Colwall CE Primary School, Malvern

Why, Why, Why Do We Have to Destroy?

I wish we wouldn't destroy,
Why, why, why do we have to destroy?
Do not destroy, save the environment, please.
Look at what you have done to the world.
Don't have wars, think of all the bombs.
Don't cut down the animals' habitats.
Let them have a life, let the poor have a home,
Please make the world a happy place.
Then you will see what the world could be like.
Maybe a better place!

Michael Goff (9)
Fitzmaurice Primary School, Bradford-on-Avon

Save The Rainforests

One day I went outside
And I saw it with my own two eyes,
Gases were floating all around
And trees were getting cut down.

> *Don't cut down the rainforest*
> *Or animals are going to die out . . .*
> *Don't cut down the rainforest*
> *Or animals are going to die out*
> *Say 'No,' say 'No,' say 'No,' say 'No,'*
> *Or animals are going to die out.*

The Earth wasn't going to last so we had to act fast,
So I went to the BBC and I got in free,
So I went upstairs to the people in red chairs,
And I showed them what was happening to the Earth,
And then they realised what they were doing,
So they organised a manager to do this job,
So he made a team to plant some seeds.

Don't cut down the rainforest
Or animals are going to die out . . .
Don't cut down the rainforest
Or animals are going to die out
Say 'No,' say 'No,' say 'No,' say 'No,'
Or animals are going to die out.

Later in the year, the rainforests grew back,
And the people cheered, the people on Earth were so happy,
They never dumped or cut down trees again.

Alex Holmes (9)
Fitzmaurice Primary School, Bradford-on-Avon

Save The Planet

Why do we make animals extinct?
Think how we would feel.
Why are we cutting down rainforests?
Please tell me, this isn't real.
Why are we leaving our TVs on standby?
We are wasting electricity.
Why are we leaving our computers on?
Don't leave our world in misery.
Our world is becoming small,
That's not a good thing is it?
We need to save electricity, not waste it.
People are running, running, inside,
Scared to take a step outside,
War is not good.
People are dropping litter on the floor,
I don't think I can take anymore.
Let's not make a habit of it.
Cans, bottles, paper, can all be recycled.
Don't go to school in a car, just cycle!
What we need are people who are good.
Listen to us children, do what you should!
Save the Earth!

Camy Rose Francis Nolan (9)
Fitzmaurice Primary School, Bradford-on-Avon

If I Were A Panda

I'm a panda - my home has gone,
I'm all alone - I have no one,
I'm so old, it's so sad,
They have killed my mother and my dad,
That makes me mad.
If I get them, I will squish them into a can,
And chuck the can into a recycle van!

Michael Dorsman (9)
Fitzmaurice Primary School, Bradford-on-Avon

If I Were Water

Sometimes I'm wasted,
Sometimes I'm not,
Sometimes I'm kept in an old pot.
I'm used for cooking,
I'm used for drinking,
But sometimes I am wasted and I think to myself,
What if I were in Africa,
Not a drop of me would be spilled.
They would smile to see a pot filled
With water, yes, delicious water.
Water, yes, delicious water.

But still I sit in my tap,
All day long,
Oh I wish I could help someone,
Who drinks from a pond.
The poor countries drink dirty water,
Whereas I am beautiful and clean.
For countries that are a bit richer,
Clean water is not a dream.

Tom Hughes (9)
Fitzmaurice Primary School, Bradford-on-Avon

Why Pollute The Earth?

I wish there were no wars, think of all the people that are so poor.
Don't cut down the trees, don't kill the trees.
Why leave TVs on standby? Think of everything that could die.
Why not recycle? Ride your bicycle.

Pollution is so bad, you could have an eco dad.
I wish there were no landfills, you might get a very expensive bill.
Animals need a life, so don't cut them with a knife.
Help to not melt the ice; if you read this poem, you've got lots of advice.

Ashley Rolt (9)
Fitzmaurice Primary School, Bradford-on-Avon

It Isn't Right

I'm flying, what fun,
There's nothing that needs to be done.
I look again at the Earth
And horror has its birth.
As I look down I see
Polluted water, the remains of a sea.
This can't be true,
The sea is supposed to be a shimmering blue.

I fly on then get a shock
For ice in the Arctic is melting by the block.
'What's doing this?' I cry,
'What is making the world so dry?'
'Pollution,' says a voice in my head.
The answer weighs me down like lead.
'This isn't happening, it isn't right,' I say,
As I look down on the Arctic white.

Kira Jukes (10)
Fitzmaurice Primary School, Bradford-on-Avon

If You Are A Wave Like Me

The waves of the sea coming over like a giant hand.
People playing and enjoying me, they come and go all the time.
When you are a wave like me, you reach up as far as you can
And just get pulled back again.
You see many wonderful things,
And some not as nice,
Like fish and more magical creatures getting trawled along,
Most already dead.
We do try to stop them but they do not.
All those fish, not used, just wasted.

    If you are a wave
            Like me!

Anna Davis (9)
Fitzmaurice Primary School, Bradford-on-Avon

No Hunters

The poor, poor things,
The animals, the bugs, so cold.
So alone,
Nowhere to go.
Why hunt? Why kill the animals?
Don't kill or hunt, please, please, don't!
This could help all the animals from becoming extinct.
Just imagine if they were doing it to us?
Why make all the fuss?
Just tell me this is just a dream,
That I'm just floating down a stream of imagination,
That it's just a mad creation.
Save the *animals!*
Save these wonderful things.
Just think, look and remember what you're doing.

Chloe Fernee (9)
Fitzmaurice Primary School, Bradford-on-Avon

What A Load Of Rubbish

Reduce this rubbish.
Reuse this rubbish.
Recycle this rubbish.
The world began because of you,
And maybe the world has a mind too.
Never mind about the landfill,
But this could be your landfill.
Just recycle this rubbish,
Just recycle it,
This rubbish could be a feature,
Also this could hurt a creature.
Look around and you will see this is the place for me.
Compost, diseases, these could be your pieces.
We must reduce, reuse, recycle.

Ellie Kettlety (9)
Fitzmaurice Primary School, Bradford-on-Avon

Wasted!

You're turning my light on, on and off,
You're wasting my energy on and off,
You're running my water on and off,
Please don't waste me, please, oh please.
Eat up your food, please, oh please.
Some people don't have any at all.
I am the world, your world, don't waste my power.
You're wasting your life, oh, don't cut it short.
All you are doing is making me hide.
You're turning my light on, on and off,
You are wasting my energy.

I, as a child, am very concerned,
Please listen to me . . . do your bit!

Chloe Townsend Williams (9)
Fitzmaurice Primary School, Bradford-on-Avon

Animals

Animals lose their babies after they are born.
Pandas are becoming extinct.
New animals die every second.
Pandas get injured and they have to be separated from their mums.
Injured pandas sometimes don't make it through surgery.
People have to look after them especially babies whose mums
have died.
These pandas get scared, they call for their mums but don't get
a call back.
As I said, animals are dying and becoming extinct.
Love our animals, love our world, please care, please.
Love our world then save our world!

Caitlin Amara Kennedy (9)
Fitzmaurice Primary School, Bradford-on-Avon

Panther

Panthers are sneaky,
Panthers are cheeky,
Crawling through the night,
They're losing their habitat,
How could you do that?
Now they're almost extinct,
In the wink of an eye,
They'll be flying by,
Up into the heavens above,
Because they have died
And gone to the skies.

Philippa Bingham (9)
Fitzmaurice Primary School, Bradford-on-Avon

Stop!

An ecological change,
A biological range
Of the bad things we've done.
And with inequality,
Then poverty,
It's not much fun.
We should make solar cars,
Not go to Mars!
Oh no, *stop!*
We're killing ourselves!

Luke Jacob Duncan (10)
Fitzmaurice Primary School, Bradford-on-Avon

Pollution

P ollution
O xygen is getting polluted
L itter
L itter
U se a bicycle
T urn off the car
I hate pollution
O h it makes me mad
N ow reduce, reuse and recycle.

Callum Giles (8)
Fitzmaurice Primary School, Bradford-on-Avon

Us

Earth is elegant, floating in cold and empty space.
Sunny, warm and bright weather.
People living in peace.
Stop, everything has turned on its head.
Homeless people living on the streets,
No food, no shelter, nothing.
Animals dying because of global warming,
Closer and closer to extinction.
All because of us!

Dominic Hewson (9)
Fitzmaurice Primary School, Bradford-on-Avon

Reduce, Reuse, Recycle

Don't drop litter, it . . .
Looks horrible
Harms animals
Destroys the planet.

Reduce, reuse, recycle . . .
It reduces landfill sites
Keeps animals alive
Helps the environment.

Ben Harris (9)
Fitzmaurice Primary School, Bradford-on-Avon

Why Is The World A Mean Place For Animals?

If there are no bees, no honey
If no owls, it will be a lonely place
So don't cut trees down, please, please, please
Be kind to Mother Nature
If there are no more big cars, imagine that
We could not change that.

Sophie Barratt (9)
Fitzmaurice Primary School, Bradford-on-Avon

Animals

Animals are losing their homes
Because lumberjacks are chopping down trees.
No one likes it
So why do they do it?
We can stop them!

Erin O'Neill (8)
Fitzmaurice Primary School, Bradford-on-Avon

The World I Created

The world I created, destroyed it you have.
The trees to chairs of your delight,
And the sea under a curse.
Steam and gas destroyed my shield.
Oh why, oh why do you destroy my life?
The work I did for you,
What happened to the world I created?
To the world I created?

Ben Brendish (9)
Fitzmaurice Primary School, Bradford-on-Avon

The Green Rap

Rainforests are burning, cabbages not growing.
It's not bad, it's worse, so help now.
Man, man, man, stop wasting electricity
Because it's bad, bad, bad.
The landfill sites are filling up,
Soon we will have to put litter on the street,
So stop littering, be
                    Green! Yo! Word!

Georgia Alexander (8)
Fitzmaurice Primary School, Bradford-on-Avon

Save Our World

L itter makes our world look like a dump.
I know we can make the world a better place.
T he world is polluting.
T ake time to recycle your rubbish.
E very day a lot of trees get cut down.
R emember, our world needs help.

Dan Holmes (7)
Fitzmaurice Primary School, Bradford-on-Avon

Standby

When my little light is on,
Everything is going wrong.
Energy is being wasted,
People are beginning to be stressed.
The world is being destroyed,
Be aware, your life is at risk.
So please, don't leave my little light on,
Because otherwise things will go wrong.

Siânel Burt (9)
Fitzmaurice Primary School, Bradford-on-Avon

Why, Oh Why?

Why, oh why
Do we pollute the sky?
Dead and extinct animals,
Be nice to mammals,
Don't leave your TV on standby,
Because I wonder,
Why, oh why,
Do we pollute the sky?

Clemmie Thompson (9)
Fitzmaurice Primary School, Bradford-on-Avon

Litter, Litter, Litter

L itter is bad for the animals.
I ncredibly bad for the environment.
T reat the environment as you like to be treated.
T ry to put the rubbish in the bin.
E veryone can make the world a better place.
R educe, reuse, recycle.

Jude McGrath (8)
Fitzmaurice Primary School, Bradford-on-Avon

Habitat

H omes of the animals
A nd the tribes
B oas are the kings of snakes
I guanas are the kings of camouflage
T igers are the kings of hunting
A ll the animals live in the rainforest
T rees are being chopped down.

Taylor Clifford-Pryer
Fitzmaurice Primary School, Bradford-on-Avon

You Can Be Eco-Friendly

Junk, litter, everywhere
All polluting the ozone layer
Climate change, polar meltdown
Animal extinction and pollution everywhere
You can be eco-friendly
You can be environmentally friendly
So please stop being a couch potato.

Eleanor Dorsman (9)
Fitzmaurice Primary School, Bradford-on-Avon

Litter

Think that every bit of litter counts.
Think about our world, you could destroy it.
God might not make a new one.
So recycle, recycle everything that can be recycled.
It all saves the world.
So next time you drop something,
Pick it up and recycle.

Harry McComish (8)
Fitzmaurice Primary School, Bradford-on-Avon

Don't Drop Litter

It's hurting the environment
Harming animals
Making the world look ugly
If you recycle you are
Helping the environment
Saving animals
Making the world look more beautiful.

Jenson Moore (8)
Fitzmaurice Primary School, Bradford-on-Avon

Rainforest Rap

Don't you hurt the little animals, yo
Or Mr Monkey's gonna get you
And what about the rainforest?
Mr Monkey and his friends aren't gonna have a home
If you chop the rainforest down.
It's easy, don't buy as much paper, yo.
And that's the end of that, yeah!

Harry Turner (9)
Fitzmaurice Primary School, Bradford-on-Avon

Rubbish

Don't chuck the rubbish on the floor.
Put it in the bin.
Use solar panels instead of heating.
Turn the TV off, not just on standby.
Do use your bikes instead of cars.
They are less polluting and it will keep you fit as well.

Rosie Ruby Binks (8)
Fitzmaurice Primary School, Bradford-on-Avon

Litter

L ooking horrible.
I f you drop litter, you will destroy the world.
T ry to be eco-friendly.
T ry to be a better person today.
E veryone needs to be responsible for the environment.
R ecycle.

Hannah Perry (8)
Fitzmaurice Primary School, Bradford-on-Avon

Litter

L itter destroys the world.
I pick up litter all the time, do you?
T idy up, put it away.
T ake care of animals, don't throw rubbish on the floor.
E verybody recycle rubbish.
R ubbish, stop throwing it on the floor, put it in the bin.

Daniel Dobroczynski (9)
Fitzmaurice Primary School, Bradford-on-Avon

Litter

L itter, don't drop litter.
I t pollutes our world.
T idy the classroom.
T ry to tidy up.
E veryone help our world now.
R euse paper.

Harry Rafferty (7)
Fitzmaurice Primary School, Bradford-on-Avon

Litter

L itter is making our world caked with rubbish.
I think dropping litter is bad.
T he world is horrid and disgusting.
T he world must be cleaner.
E arth needs to be cleaner than it already is.
R ubbish is taking over our world!

Harriet Lock
Fitzmaurice Primary School, Bradford-on-Avon

Will You Ever Be The Same?

You were my friend, my light to my path.
You brought me up to this day.
Look at you now, you are nothing to me anymore.
You tear me apart, you drive tears down my face.
Are you my light to my path? It's not right!
Will you ever be the same?

Chere Yee Law (9)
Fitzmaurice Primary School, Bradford-on-Avon

Litter

L ots of things are going to waste.
I t's incredible how much litter there is.
T ry to put it in the bin.
T he landfill sites are filling up.
E nvironment is dying.
R emember these things next time you drop something.

Anna Gilbert (8)
Fitzmaurice Primary School, Bradford-on-Avon

Litterbug

L itter is making the world stinky.
I think we should help our world.
T ime to think about our world.
T hink about our world now.
E arth needs help!
R ight! It's time to help our world.

Regan Campbell (7)
Fitzmaurice Primary School, Bradford-on-Avon

Look After Our Planet

L ook after our planet.
I t is beautiful.
T he planet is cool.
T he world we live in is wonderful.
E arth is excellent.
R ecycle your rubbish.

Mark Saxby
Fitzmaurice Primary School, Bradford-on-Avon

Litter, Litter Everywhere

L itter is getting worse and worse
I hate litter, because it is everywhere.
T ake care of our world.
T ake care to use the bins; use both sides of the paper.
E asy on the paper.
R educe, reuse, recycle, the 3 Rs.

Martin Mander (7)
Fitzmaurice Primary School, Bradford-on-Avon

Litter

L itter is bad to dump on the ground.
I think we should stop wasting food.
T reat our planet nicely.
T hink about electricity.
E lectricity is being wasted.
R ubbish is a dump.

Amelie Butt (7)
Fitzmaurice Primary School, Bradford-on-Avon

Litter

L ouis hates litter.
I hate litter.
T he Earth helps.
T he Earth is brilliant.
E arth is good.
R ecycle all paper.

Louis Fernee (7)
Fitzmaurice Primary School, Bradford-on-Avon

Litter

L itter is bad.
I t is good to recycle.
T idy our environment.
T ake care not to drop your litter.
E very day food gets wasted.
R ubbish is taking over landfill sites.

Corey Veasey (7)
Fitzmaurice Primary School, Bradford-on-Avon

Litter

L itter is bad, it's taking over the Earth.
I n the world, the environment is becoming unhealthy.
T he world is becoming unhealthy.
T he world is getting worse day by day.
E nough is enough.
R ubbish is not good for us!

James Chivers (7)
Fitzmaurice Primary School, Bradford-on-Avon

Litter, Litter Everywhere

L itter is bad for the environment and
I s disgusting, especially for the animals.
T idy up our world as much as possible.
T idy up now, otherwise animals will become extinct.
E arth is getting hotter, so don't use so much electricity.
R ubbish is taking over, so tidy up now!

Abby Ellis (7)
Fitzmaurice Primary School, Bradford-on-Avon

Litter

L itter can kill.
I hate nasty, gross litter.
T reat the world nicely.
T ry to chuck your litter in the bin.
E vil to litter everywhere.
R ecycle litter.

Jordan Ludlam (7)
Fitzmaurice Primary School, Bradford-on-Avon

What A Load Of Rubbish

L itter is polluting our world, we need to stop it.
I am going to help the world to be a better place.
T he world is horrid and disgusting now.
T he world will be cool and fresh.
E arth is the most important thing to us.
R ubbish throwing is becoming a habit.

William Holmes (7)
Fitzmaurice Primary School, Bradford-on-Avon

Litter

L itter is bad.
I t traps animals.
T he people who drop rubbish are bad.
T here is loads of litter on the floor.
E veryone hates litter.
R ound the litter goes.

Taylor Graywood (8)
Fitzmaurice Primary School, Bradford-on-Avon

Litter

L itter is bad for the world. Please don't drop it.
I t is bad for the world.
T he world is like a dump with all the litter.
T he litter is bad for animals.
E very day people drop rubbish.
R ubbish is bad to drop.

Lewis Kettlety (7)
Fitzmaurice Primary School, Bradford-on-Avon

Litter

L itter is taking over the world.
I am very worried about it.
T he Earth is in danger.
T he poor animals that are going to become extinct.
E lin and me make litter into something new.
R ubbish tips are too full!

Tristyn Lee (7)
Fitzmaurice Primary School, Bradford-on-Avon

What A Load Of Rubbish

L itter is bad because it pollutes.
I mprove the world by recycling rubbish.
T reat the world in a good way.
T ackle litter.
E ncourage people to recycle.
R educe, reuse, recycle!

Matthew Smart (8)
Fitzmaurice Primary School, Bradford-on-Avon

Litter

L itter is bad for our world
I t's bad for the environment
T he world needs help
T he world is turning into a dump
E ach piece of litter you pick up makes a difference
R educe, reuse, recycle.

Kate Blowers (6)
Fitzmaurice Primary School, Bradford-on-Avon

Earth

E arth is dying.
A nimals are in danger.
R educe, reuse, recycle.
T he ice caps are melting.
H elp, the rainforest is being destroyed.

Louis Judge-Hodkinson (9)
Fitzmaurice Primary School, Bradford-on-Avon

Don't Pollute

Don't pollute or dump things anywhere,
because if our ozone layer goes,
we will not be allowed outside because of the heat.
So don't throw anything on the ground
Or our lives will be boring, so don't pollute!

Jack Stacey (10)
Fitzmaurice Primary School, Bradford-on-Avon

Rainforest Animals

Animals are losing their homes every day.
It's like the animals taking our homes away.
Would you like animals destroying our homes?
So why do we take their homes?
So stop before it's too late.

Emerald Lumbard-McCarthy (8)
Fitzmaurice Primary School, Bradford-on-Avon

Reduce, Reuse, Recycle

Always pick up litter
Whenever you see it.
Don't just ignore it.
Keep your world clean and tidy.
Reduce the amount of litter you throw.

Charlotte Lomax Turner (8)
Fitzmaurice Primary School, Bradford-on-Avon

Beautiful Planet

Look at the world around us,
What do you see?
A beautiful planet
Or a mess made by you and me?

We need to save our planet
Before it is too late,
Everyone can make a difference,
C'mon, let's make it great!

Reduce, reuse, recycle,
It's as easy as one, two, three,
Don't use too much paper,
It will help to save a tree.

So now I've got you thinking,
You see it's not so strange,
The smallest bit of effort,
Can make a massive change.

Callum Farmer (7)
Great Rissington Primary School, Cheltenham

Be Eco

B e eco. Do not pollute rivers, seas and streams.
E co is cool. Our school is eco-friendly.

E veryone should try to be eco.
C ool is being eco.
O ur planet needs to be saved.

E co is what I do.
V ery eco our school is.
E ach one of us needs to reduce, reuse, recycle.
R eady, steady, be eco!
Y es, we do try.
W e do not waste electricity.
H eavy boats pollute the seas.
E co is important.
R ight, we have to do it now.
E co, eco is fabulous.

Bethan McGuinness-Dean (8)
Great Rissington Primary School, Cheltenham

Be Eco

Want to be green?
Don't be mean,
Save the grass,
Recycle your glass.

You don't have to be a teen
To be eco green.
Young or old, big or small,
We can learn to reuse it all.

Don't get in a flap
With your piles of scrap.
There are ways and means
Of being eco green.

Alexander Winter (8)
Great Rissington Primary School, Cheltenham

Be An Eco·School

Be an eco-school and try to get the eco-flag,
Eco-schools can save trees and avoid the plastic bag.

All our food from local suppliers,
Not for us overseas fliers.

Electricity is precious, turn off the lights!
Conserve water, shallow baths not brimming heights,
Organic matter, paper, glass and plastic.

Save, recycle, it's not so drastic.
Cycle to school, enjoy the fresh air,
Harness the wind, show you care,
Observe the rules; we should all try to be green,
Only we can keep our planet clean,
Love life!

Helen Gray (7)
Great Rissington Primary School, Cheltenham

Eco

I went to my wood,
A man was cutting down the trees,
I said to the man,
'Don't cut them down please.'

Trees are homes
For creatures big and small,
And if you chop trees,
They'll have no home at all!

If we don't waste paper,
And we leave the trees alone,
The world will be greener
And the Earth a better home.

Nell Kate Venables (6)
Great Rissington Primary School, Cheltenham

Eco Poem

Save the paper
Then save the trees.
Save the planet
For the birds and bees.

Save electricity
Then save the sky.
Save the animals
So they don't die.

Save the rubbish
Then save the sea.
Save the people
And you and me.

Sophie Brown (6)
Great Rissington Primary School, Cheltenham

Eco Poem

I was taught to be green
I was taught to buy local beans
I was told to reduce
I was told to reuse
I was told to recycle forever
I have to turn off lights
I have to turn off computers
I have to turn off the TV every day
I know how to save water
I know how to grow veg
I know how to be green
I know to be green forever.

Felicity Darwent (7)
Great Rissington Primary School, Cheltenham

A Lovely Eco-Day

If you stop things from dying
You can go flying
Get the eco-flag
It's no ordinary rag
Make sure you don't waste trees
Or you will get chased by giant bees
Don't be lazy
Or we will call you daily
Don't pollute
Or it will cost you loot
Be an eco-school
Or you won't get a free pool.

Miles Regan Beard (7)
Great Rissington Primary School, Cheltenham

Planet Earth

P lanet Earth is becoming a mess.
L earn to reduce, reuse, recycle.
A n eco-friendly world will make people smile.
N ow we should all do our bit.
E verybody should be an eco-warrior.
T ry to share cars with other people.

E arth needs our help.
A lways turn electric things off if you're not using them.
R educe paper waste - use both sides of your paper.
T his will make our environment healthy.
H elp spread the word!

Harrison Adsett (7)
Great Rissington Primary School, Cheltenham

Help To Be Green

Help the eco planet,
Save our world,
Help the trees, yes us, you and me!
Recycle paper, do your job,
Help save electricity.
Save our plants,
Save our water, make us smile,
Don't let up, don't be lazy,
Help the seas and the bees.
Love the days, turn out the lights,
Swap your car for an eco bike.

Antonia Beeching (6)
Great Rissington Primary School, Cheltenham

Turn The Earth Back

L ong ago, before Man came,
E verything was beautiful on the Earth.
T hen Man came but didn't think and
S poiled the Earth with waste and pollution.

H ow can we make things right?
E veryone needs to help heal our planet.
L et's turn the Earth back
P lease.

Marcus Kiey-Thomas (7)
Great Rissington Primary School, Cheltenham

Let's

Let's save the world
Let's help animals
Let's be green
Let's be eco-friendly
Let's not cut down trees
Let's buy local food
Let's recycle
Let's have fun doing it.

Alice Poole (7)
Great Rissington Primary School, Cheltenham

Eco·Poem

Be eco, help the world grow, grow, grow
Help the plants and be an eco-school
Recycle, reduce, reuse paper and cardboard
Save trees and bees
Turn off the lights when you have finished!
I like being green
So I think we could save the world
Plant a seed and let it grow into a tree.

Lucy Guy (7)
Great Rissington Primary School, Cheltenham

Be Eco

B e careful not to waste paper.
E at local food.

E nergy is precious, use it wisely.
C ompost fruit and vegetables.
O ften recycle as much as you can.

Ben Sedgwick (7)
Great Rissington Primary School, Cheltenham

Eco·Poem

Save green trees and little bees.
Turn lights off.
Reduce and recycle.
Be eco-friendly.
Turn taps off.
Be an eco-school and follow the rule.
Fly an eco-flag made from a bag.

Harriet Adams (6)
Great Rissington Primary School, Cheltenham

Eco Poem

Eco, eco, the world is great
eco, eco, the world is big
the world is funny
the world is sunny
we will not waste paper
otherwise our world
will not be very nice at all.

Alex Hope (6)
Great Rissington Primary School, Cheltenham

Eco·Poem

Reduce: We reduce packaging by using our own bags.
We reduce water consumption by turning the tap off when brushing our teeth.

Reuse: Using rechargeable batteries.

Recycle: Putting things in the right bins for the binmen to recycle.
Water butts recycle rainwater.

Lucy Blackwell-Cronie (6)
Great Rissington Primary School, Cheltenham

45

Eco·Poem

Green is best
so please clear your mess.

Recycle your plastic, paper and card.
Don't leave it lying in your backyard.

Let's do it together
for the *world!*

Edward Gum (7)
Great Rissington Primary School, Cheltenham

Be Eco

B ees are dying
E lephants are crying
E nergy should be saved

E veryone stop and think
C ans, use the recycle bin
O ur world is dying.

Nathaniel Payne (9)
Great Rissington Primary School, Cheltenham

Eco·Poem

B e eco everyone
E arth is in danger

E veryone, put bottles in the recycling bins
C are for the world and save the animals
O n the way to getting the eco-flag!

Emily Yates (9)
Great Rissington Primary School, Cheltenham

Be Eco·Friendly

Bees are dying.
Elephants are crying.

Eco is the best.
Come on, do it.
On the way to triumph.

Alastair Gleghorn (8)
Great Rissington Primary School, Cheltenham

Eco Poem

You have to not waste paper
And you have to use the paper on both sides
You have to eat good food and not eat horrid food.
You have to make houses for animals
And put out hedgehog houses.

Jamie Lord (6)
Great Rissington Primary School, Cheltenham

Green

G o green!
R euse, reduce, recycle!
E verybody save the planet!
E ach of us makes a difference!
N ow go green!

Grace Walsingham (7)
Great Rissington Primary School, Cheltenham

Eco·Poem

Recycling is good,
you must protect
all the wood,
and then everything
will be as it should.

Maria Dickman (6)
Great Rissington Primary School, Cheltenham

Eco·Poem

Let's be green, let's be clean.
Don't throw rubbish on to the green.
Let's not pollute our shoots or roots.

Archie Sumner (6)
Great Rissington Primary School, Cheltenham

Green Acrostic

G reen
R ecycling is
E xcellent
E nthusiastic
N ot throwing rubbish on the ground.

E nvironment would like you to recycle
C ans need recycling
O ur world needs your help!

James David Lucas (7)
Leehurst Swan School, Salisbury

Our Wonderful World

Our world is being destroyed
And some species of animals are becoming extinct,
Don't let this happen!
We need to rethink!
It makes me feel secure.
It sounds like singing birds,
It feels solid,
It looks extraordinary,
It smells fabulous.

If we let this happen
We won't have anything on our planet,
We won't be alive
And nothing will be,
We need help if we are to survive.

Oscar Ho (8)
Leehurst Swan School, Salisbury

Turn Off The Light

Always remember
to turn off the light
so it's not on all night.
Alright?

Turn off the light!

Ottilie Knight (7)
Leehurst Swan School, Salisbury

49

The Tree That Tells You What To Do

Save paper
Recycle paper
Reuse paper
Don't drop litter.

Luca Ho (8)
Leehurst Swan School, Salisbury

Recycling · Haiku

Recycling is good
Help save our environment
Turn off the tap now.

Ruby Cooper (7)
Leehurst Swan School, Salisbury

Eco World · Haiku

Hey! Be smart, be green
Recycle stuff - it is cool!
Save the Earth for all!

Sam Higson (7)
Leehurst Swan School, Salisbury

Flowers

There are so many flowers in the whole wide world,
Pink, yellow, orange, purple, blue and green,
If you try to kill them you are so mean,
So work together to keep the environment clean.

Ellie Marsh (11) & Jamie Kneen (10))
Murray's Road School, Douglas

The Green Poem

When you're walking down the street,
Just look down at your feet.
If you see a plastic can,
Don't throw it at a van,
Don't do a deadly sin
Just put it in the bin!

When you're in the school day
Whether work or play,
And you're standing in the line
Remember look at the sign.
Switch the light off,
Or you might just get a cough!

When you're sitting at home,
Playing with your gnome,
Having lots of fun,
With your hair in a bun,
Don't leave your TV on,
Or the world will soon be gone!

Isobel Johnson & Amy Kinley (10)
Murray's Road School, Douglas

Litterbugs

L itter affects nature
I 'll be picking it up
T hink before you do it
T he litter cannot walk
E at your food, put the rubbish in the bin
R ubbish does not live on the floor
B ugs die because they eat our litter
U ntidy world!
G ood people don't litter
S o try to be a good person.

Keera Hooper & Hannah Selman (9)
Parkwall Primary School, Cadbury Heath

Make The World Better

Recycle in the green bin
It's like the world's got to spin
Switch off, not on standby
Or kiss the world goodbye.
We've all got to work together
To make the world better
Don't cut down a tree
Listen to the buzzy bee
Treat the world with respect
This poem is here to help,
Now who's with me?

Katie Apthorpe (10)
Parkwall Primary School, Cadbury Heath

Recycling Rubbish

R otten rubbish
E nds up in the bins
C rushed into tiny flakes
Y et it starts a new life
C oming to the shops
L oving the bumpy ride
I n the back of the van
N ot alone anymore
G oing to a new home.

Gemma Lane (9)
Parkwall Primary School, Cadbury Heath

Rubbish

R ubbish is messy
U ntidy
B ooms into the waterfall
B angs into the rocks
I ncredible
S melly
H orrible.

Jade Henderson (9)
Parkwall Primary School, Cadbury Heath

Recycle

R ecycle your cans
E veryone can do it
C an we save the planet?
Y ou can help too
C an we do it?
L earn about the planet
E veryone can do it.

Lewis Ricketts (9)
Parkwall Primary School, Cadbury Heath

Waste

Recycle all your tins and cans
Then you'll have lots of fans
Ride your bike to school each day
Then for petrol you don't pay
Don't leave your phone on charge overnight
It might give the environment a fright!

Lily Rawcliffe (9)
Parkwall Primary School, Cadbury Heath

Litter

If you want to live longer
Listen to this rhyme
We know it's already in your mind
So start to look left and look right
Make sure that there is no litter in sight.
If there is, then pick it up
Then the world won't look a scruff,
Recycle hard
Recycle more
Make sure that you do it all.
Pick it up
Put it in
Make sure it's always in the recycle bin.
Littering is a serious crime
Think twice about it.

Or you could get a fine!

James Rafferty (11)
St Joseph's RC Primary School, Billingham

On The Streets

What do I do?
Where do I go?
I'm out on the street
Stood shivering, cold.

The wind it howls
The rain it pours
There's no one there
No open doors.

I've lost it all
There's not a sound
My heart is cold
My stomach torn
Oh, what a senseless deadly war.

Narelle Barkes (10)
St Joseph's RC Primary School, Billingham

Pollution

Pollution makes our planet sad,
Pollution makes everything bad,
Unwanted smells that really stink
Doesn't that just make you think
That the Earth could be a better place?
And without all the rubbish
There would be lots more space!
So remember to put that empty tin
Into the nearest rubbish bin
Help us make our world a better place
That will last forever for the whole Human Race.

Jack Ross, Shkira Lal, Leonie Wills, Joseph Foster, Cameron Kelly, Georgia Fleming, Austen-James Long, Megan Marsh, Jim Smith, Chloe Francis, Oliver McHale & Charlotte Weepers (6-10)
St Joseph's RC Primary School, Billingham

The Rockpool

I found a little rockpool
Shining in display
So pretty like a spider's web in the torrential rain.
Then I saw the lifeless fish
Floating and floating gently
I shouted, 'Help! Help!' But no one heard me!
I ran to my mother, told her the truth.
And she looked at the rockpool
And she shook her head.
She told me about pollution
And how the world was bad
For dumping horrible litter in the sea.
Rivers, ponds and even ocean wide!
Never again will I be a litterbug
And I'll tell my friends this too
That I'll be watching *you!*

Tamsyn Tuburu (9)
St Margaret's CE Primary School, Durham

Monsoon

It slashes through open windows
It drowns the crops mercilessly,
This is the storm,
Devastation fills the air
It whips at people's faces
Animals scatter left and right
It brings so much darkness
The sun has to cry.
The sound of the angry wind booms all around.
It rips open homes
And floods the village with despair.
This is the storm that takes
So many lives.
And we're the people that can help.

Tamsyn Tuburu (9)
St Margaret's CE Primary School, Durham

Dustbin Saves The world

Hello my name is Dustbin.
I have two wheels that
Can save the world.
I work all day, I run
Around like a headless
Chicken, picking litter up.
When the litter is all gone,
A smile comes upon my face.
The amount of litter
Spoils my view.
Half an hour later the view is perfect.
Shut doors, save heating, turn lights off,
Save the sun.
Yippee!

Alex Wood (8)
St Mary's RC Primary School, Eccles

My World, Your World, Our World

World at war,
World no soul,
World no heart,
World explode.

Bombs explode,
People die,
Families heartbroken,
Children cry.

World No Soul?

Glass bottles,
Tin cans
Plastic bags,
Made by man.

World No Heart?

Other countries,
People suffer,
War effects,
Food is scarce.
Working labour,
Not much pay,
Will they survive another day?

World Explode?

World tomorrow,
World today,
Let's act now,
Let's live another day!

World at war,
World no soul,
World no heart,
World explode?

Hannah Cunliffe (10)
St Mary's RC Primary School, Eccles

Recycle, Reduce, Reuse

Cans, bottles, and lots lots more,
All of them being thrown on the floor
Looking after the Earth, it's going poor,
Litter, graffiti, it happens all the more.

Saving the Earth may be a bore,
But come on people, we can do more!
Trees, rainforests, they're being cut down,
Help recycle, tell the whole town!

Gas, electric, the tale's the same,
Don't use it up, this isn't a game.
Come on tell us what do you think?
Do you really want the world to reek and stink?
Cycle to work, walk to school,
Whether it's hot or whether it's cold.
Come on, don't be a sore thumb,
Save the world now and it'll get done.

If you throw rubbish on the floor,
You'll get a ticket, darn right, sure.
Save the world, save it now,
Or else the ozone layer will come right down.
Stop pollution, do it for real,
Or you may not see your next meal!

Think of the ozone layer, don't bring it down,
Look at the Earth, it's got a big frown.
The Earth is back and whole again,
And now he is your friend again.

Cameron Pearce (10)
St Mary's RC Primary School, Eccles

Save The World!

The world is in danger,
And it's all down to us.
If we don't do something now,
We are out with a bang!

We can start by using less cars,
They let out deadly fumes,
But if you listen, you'll understand,
It's better to take the bus.

Litter is a real problem,
It makes the place a mess,
But don't just throw things away
Let's try to recycle!
Graffiti, graffiti, graffiti,
Will youngsters ever learn?
They think it makes them bad and hard,
They don't have a clue!

War is just wrong,
It's too dangerous and pointless
Soldiers earn lots of money!
To put their lives at risk.

All this is terrible,
It's doing us harm.
We are polluting the Earth
And it's got out of hand!

Callum Brookes (10)
St Mary's RC Primary School, Eccles

The Bang!

Floors will crackle,
The homes will fall,
The Earth will blow,
The schools will go.

If you're greedy,
I am sure,
That the air we breathe will be poor.
The sun was able to shine,
Through the ozone's line
The trees will fly away,
The Earth will die,
That binman is why.

Recycle, recycle, recycle,
Brown is plastic,
Green is bottles,
Pink is gardening,
Black is for the world to come to
            An end!

Lucy Davies (10)
St Mary's RC Primary School, Eccles

Rubbish, Rubbish!

Paper, paper, rubbish, paper and cans are rubbish!
Put into bins and not on the streets!
Cans go in brown bins and paper goes in blue bins.
Rubbish, rubbish put into bins
And then you will see what will happen to your world!
Recycle! Recycle the possibilities are endless!
Paper is good, but not on the streets,
It can ruin our lives.
            Remember to recycle . . .
                  Trees!

James Cartwright (10)
St Mary's RC Primary School, Eccles

Help!

Trees, trees
Beautiful reeds,
Growing fruits, is what they do
Making some food for our whole planet,
Giving us oxygen to have good air
But what will happen if they're cut down?
Nobody knows until it's done.

All types of weather
All mixed together,
No more sun and no more rain
But hurricane and storm instead,
What will happen if this was true?
Nobody knows until it's too late.

Paper, paper rubbish maker
No more trees will mean no fruit.
But if this is true
What shall we do?

Ed Chester G Martinez (10)
St Mary's RC Primary School, Eccles

Litter Is So Bitter

Where there is litter
It looks so bitter
Everywhere I go
I say, 'No, no, no.'
Cans, bottles, anything more,
Recycle them all so they're not on the floor.
Because it is there
The world can't bear another second to live
So please just give
The time to stop
Before we all go *pop!*

Alysia Kavanagh (10)
St Mary's RC Primary School, Eccles

Save The Animals

Make this world a better place
And not a big disgrace.
Keep this world a better place,
Keep it tidy and don't make it dirty.
Make our planet green and clear.
Make our planet clean and clear.
Let's keep walking, walking, walk,
Don't keep talking, talk, talk, talk.

You can walk to school, it is not really far,
So why would you need the car?
Let's turn off the light when you're done,
To save the energy from the sun.

Keep the water fresh and clean
So the creatures can stay in the sea.

Save Eccles, keep it clean
And let's be green.

Tori-Eileen Young (8)
St Mary's RC Primary School, Eccles

The Big Recycle Man

Making everything green
Is what I do.
Saving sea creatures,
Saving the environment
Is what I do.
By turning off
The light,
Not shining like Buckingham Palace.
Soon it will be completed
By the recycling man.

John Royle (8)
St Mary's RC Primary School, Eccles

Save Our World

Let's stop polluting
And all the shooting
And make our world a better place
Let's get new flowers
And put them right.

Let's stop the war
And all the hurting
And make our world a better place
Let's tell everyone to
Just make friends
And we can all live a happy life.

Let's stop the graffiti
And all the spray paint
And make our world a better place
Let's get new walls
And keep them clean.

Ashleigh Richardson (10)
St Mary's RC Primary School, Eccles

Clean Clean

Hello I am Mr Clean.
I am the cleanest in the town.
Your house should be clean too
And the whole wide world should be clean.
Clean, clean, I clean dustbins and everything else that is dirty.
Hello again I am Mr Clean,
I have really fast and zooming wheels,
So I can go really fast.
Clean, clean, clean, everyone likes me and I like myself too.
Come on everybody, let's get cleaning,
You're not tired are you?
No, then lets go and clean.

Jithin Saju (8)
St Mary's RC Primary School, Eccles

Recycle

Recycle, recycle
Go to school on a cycle.
Keep the world clean
And definitely not mean.
Make the world green
So when you recycle you will be keen.
It should be a better place
It must look like a mushroom's face
It's good to fly kites
But not to fire dynamites.
If you like black
That means you have a bumpy back.
So have it sunny
You will earn lots of money.
That's all for now
I will see you in the next town.

Davidson Sabu (8)
St Mary's RC Primary School, Eccles

The World Of Clean And Green

Turn off lights when you're done,
Go outside and use the sun.
Dance, and jive, and have some fun.
We're saving energy and we're not done.

We need a super litter machine
That picks up cans from where they have been.
Start getting keen to make our world green,
Type in the eco-code and you're an eco-queen.

You and I will save our world,
Don't let litter go to waste.
Just recycle it, it will appear again
As a different thing.

Lucy Chester (8)
St Mary's RC Primary School, Eccles

Stop Poverty!

Some people don't have money
Some people don't have food
Some people don't have homes
Some people don't have anything
But why?
Everyone should have this
Everyone can.

Don't be selfish
Donate to charity
Don't waste food
Give to the hungry
Don't be cruel
Help people to build homes
Don't throw away things
Give what's not wanted to the unfortunate.

Matthew Houten (10)
St Mary's RC Primary School, Eccles

Save Our Animals And World

You should be keen
On making our world green.
Lots of litter on the ground
Endangering sea creatures in the ocean.
Litter thrown all around,
Don't pollute rivers nearby,
It's not good for the environment.

Walk to places,
Don't be lazy
Even though you have heavy cases.
Now make a start on making our town green.
Recycle litter don't let it go to waste.
Don't let resources go to waste.

Lauryn Leigh Brown (9)
St Mary's RC Primary School, Eccles

Save Our World

Don't waste paper
Don't take away our oxygen
Recycle it please
Save our world!

Don't drive
Walk, get exercise
Help save our world!

Don't litter
Don't leave your dog poo
On the floor,
Save our world.

Don't kill
Make peace
Save our world!

Charlie Mannion (10)
St Mary's RC Primary School, Eccles

My Eco·Poem

Keep our world clean and green!
Don't make a big and black disgrace.
Keep it clean, keep it green,
And keep it cool and sometimes cold.

Get out the car, don't pollute!
If you do, I will hate you!
Keep the grass, don't freak out,
And don't break your bones.

Keep your friend, don't fall out
It's not fair to each other.
Don't throw stones, it might hurt -
Also don't throw leaves, they might hurt.

Charlotte Hockham-Edge (8)
St Mary's RC Primary School, Eccles

A Better Place

If you want to make our world a better place,
You cannot make a mistake,
The trees are being cut down,
Because of our selfishness!
Do not let it happen! Recycle!

Our world is about to explode!
The ozone layer is getting smashed,
Think if it happens because of us
Don't throw cans on the floor,
If it carries on . . .
        Bang!
        The earth will have exploded!

Artur Boruc (11)
St Mary's RC Primary School, Eccles

Turn It Off Turn It On

Turn it off, turn it on
But turn it off when not needed or gone.
Make our world a better place
Let's not make it a disgrace.
Throw your rubbish in the bin
Because sea creatures can get caught.
Then you will be taught.

Use the paper, use it all
Or the heap will become far beyond tall.

Keep our world green
Let's not be mean.

Stacey O'Neill (8)
St Mary's RC Primary School, Eccles

Cleaning The Bin

Hello my name is Cleany,
We need to save the world
So don't throw litter over the clean floor.

If I am half full, I know that there is litter on the floor.
Recycle, recycle, please recycle,
Reuse paper, please recycle glass, paper, plastic
And other things.

Turn off the lights when you are finished,
Don't leave them on.

Kieron Marshall (8)
St Mary's RC Primary School, Eccles

Dump

Dump, dump, dumping, people are littering
And cleaners are wasting their time.
You're wrecking the atmosphere
People are getting poorly, people are throwing it in the sea.
Fish are dying.

People are getting germs, the world will soon be dirty,
People are throwing things in the bin,
People are picking litter up.
People are doing the right things . . .

Joey Smith (8)
St Mary's RC Primary School, Eccles

Pollution Resolution

Hate pollution
I've got a solution
You can recycle
Or ride a bicycle
If you cut all the trees down
You're giving Earth an even bigger frown
We need oxygen so keep our trees
All these things are not just saving me,
They are saving the world.

Thomas Vale (10)
St Mary's RC Primary School, Eccles

Follow The Eco·Code

Keep our world
Just like your bedroom
Don't throw litter on the floor
Recycling is the best thing to do.

Don't put rubbish in the sea
It will kill the sea creatures.
Don't put rubbish in the school,
The teachers will fall.

Roisin Murton (8)
St Mary's RC Primary School, Eccles

The Forest

We bring oxygen day and night
Animals nest in our branches
When we are together we make a beautiful sight
But when you cut us all down you will end up with a big fright
Recycle paper that's the solution,
We stand tall to feel the pitter-patter of rain on our leaves,
Then if we keep you alive, why do you still hurt us?

Joe Hickey (10)
St Mary's RC Primary School, Eccles

The Big Green Poetry Machine

Storms are getting stronger
Countries are becoming warmer
This is the Earth changing
Because of our own doing.

Our animals are becoming extinct
Because forests are starting to shrink
Plants and trees are dying
And we should stop this happening.

We should all start to reduce and reuse,
Like turn off the lights when not in use
Everyone should always recycle
And save energy like using your own bicycle.

If we all do this
Our earth would be pleased
And it would be a nicer place to live
And always remember to always help and give.

Ken Quirante (10)
St Richard's Catholic Primary School, Skelmersdale

Bad Things In The World

War is bad and so sad, war breaks people's hearts,
So deadly, so much danger for a normal ranger.
Recycling is good, not as good as it could.
Every person should recycle because it helps to save the environment,
And probably the world.
Someday those who don't recycle
Will pay for what they will do and they have done.
That's why you should quit on CO_2.
All you have to do is turn off your tap when not in use.
Turn the TV off when not in use, even when the red light is on,
It still uses electricity.
That is all you have to do to save energy.
All the animals will be dead if you don't turn lights off when you go to bed.
Climate change will kill, so silent, so still,
Water levels will rise and cause floods on all the coast around the country.
This will only take about 50 years to take place
Lives will be lost and that's what will happen
If we don't stop climate change.
Disease is so tragic, so painful, so hurtful,
Thousands of people die a day because of disease,
The worst disease that is going around is called AIDS.
Most people catch this in poorer parts of the world.

Andrew Larkin (10)
St Richard's Catholic Primary School, Skelmersdale

Let's Recycle

Recycling is really, really great
The environment is the most important place
Pollution is very, very bad
Give the world love and more to add.

Alan McKinnell (11)
St Richard's Catholic Primary School, Skelmersdale

Global Warming

What has happened to our Earth?
There's no new life, no one's giving birth.
There are no birds, there are no trees
There is no land; only seas.
Swamped houses and flooded towns,
I bet this image is giving you frowns!
This is a future, I don't want to see,
It's time for a change, you and me.
Recycle rubbish when you can,
Help save our fellowman.
Wash your clothes on a lower setting
Or this is the future we will be getting.
Everyone act now, don't delay
Or this vision may be on its way.
Make the change now, listen to the warning,
Or this is reality - global warming.

Cain Gaudie (10)
St Richard's Catholic Primary School, Skelmersdale

Keeping Green!

We're very keen
On keeping green,
These ideas will show what I mean,
Recycling can be a chore, but then again it does make more,
Walk instead of using the car,
It's probably not even that far,
Wash our clothes by low degrees,
It will keep the polar ice caps a-freeze,
Flick off the switch,
One day you may be rich,
Now you all know what I mean,
Come on everybody, it's easy,
        Let's turn green!

Ellis O'Brien (10)
St Richard's Catholic Primary School, Skelmersdale

What's Wrong?

Littering is bad,
Oh you know you shouldn't have
Left that rubbish on the floor,
Please don't do that anymore
Because it makes me sad.

Pollution is not good.
I really wish you would
Stop leaking oil into the sea,
Causing a catastrophe
For all the animals in the 'hood.

Don't throw them away,
Recycle! Think about who could play
With your old and used toys.
Pass them onto the girls and boys
And really make their day.

Ben West (10)
St Richard's Catholic Primary School, Skelmersdale

Stop The War

Stop the war, war is bad,
It kills your mum and dad.
If you don't stop the war,
You will destroy the Earth and more.
Please stop, it's not good,
Please, please, you really should.

Don't fight,
Settle down,
Don't do it,
For a crown,
Get on together,
It'll be very clever.

James Mitchell (9)
St Richard's Catholic Primary School, Skelmersdale

Homeless

It is not something we like to see,
People living in poverty,
No money for food, rent or clothes,
They move to the subways in their droves,
With a box, a blanket, and a dog for company.
Is this the best we can offer in this once great country?

In times of need can we spare a 'dime'?
But in truth we don't even spare them our 'time'.
The loneliness, the dampness, the freezing cold,
This is not the tale that Thatcher told.
When we moan and groan in our everyday lives
And we cheat and like to get everything new,
Spare a kind thought for those poor souls
Who are out there selling the 'Big Issue'.

Alex Beamer (11)
St Richard's Catholic Primary School, Skelmersdale

Treat The World As A Gift!

The world was given to us as a gift
As we flick through story books,
We always see colourful illustrations
Of the world, at its best,
But that's not what I see,
I see chewing gum upon the pavement floor,
Newspaper gliding through the air and across the road.
Empty cans sitting on fences,
Initials written in felt-tip on the brick wall,
Should it be this way?
Is this the way you want to live?
I know I don't.
Let's get together, young people, and make our world cleaner,
Safer and more importantly, a nice place to live.

Lauren Procter (11)
St Richard's Catholic Primary School, Skelmersdale

It's Mean Not To Go Green

It's mean not to go green,
Rainforests suffer, we suffer
We bring this on ourselves,
Animals close to extinction
To one great big disease for killing,
As we do, our bet to pollute the planet,
And cutting down trees and causing disease.
Our wish to succeed in life,
And suffering to some along the way,
With some being homeless,
Also the world wishes to cause problems,
With the world at war that nobody wins in the end.

Laura Beesley (10)
St Richard's Catholic Primary School, Skelmersdale

Stop Polluton

Look at the dirty rotten sea,
Not a nice sight to see,
You can' see the bottom,
Because it's all rotten.
We can't even swim in it,
Did you tip your bin in it?
The sand we can't walk on,
All the pleasure is gone,
Act now
Stop pollution.

Ellie Coakley (11)
St Richard's Catholic Primary School, Skelmersdale

Eco Poem

Litter picker
Plant grower
Earth saver
Green fingers
Plant feeder
Lolly licker
Plant fixer

What am I
Eco-kid.

Alex Bennett (10)
St Richard's Catholic Primary School, Skelmersdale

Petrol Fumes

If we drive to school, it melts our ice caps.
This is caused by petrol fumes which are going into the air
And causing the climate to change.
The polar caps are melting, so the sea is rising higher,
If we don't act now we will not have enough time to act,
Think of the future,
There may not be one,
So use less of the car,
And more of your feet.

Jarrod Lea (10)
St Richard's Catholic Primary School, Skelmersdale

Fast Food

Men with chainsaws
Cutting down trees
To make more room
For cows to graze
Fast food
Fast food
Cutting down trees
We have to make sure
The rainforest stays.

Tom Holcroft (10)
St Richard's Catholic Primary School, Skelmersdale

Litter

Don't drop me
In the sea.
In the bin,
Is not a sin.
Crisp packets,
Bottle tops,
Even dirty washing mops,
If you want a smiley grin,
Put me in the garbage bin.

Ryan Geraghty (9)
St Richard's Catholic Primary School, Skelmersdale

Can You Help Recycle?

R ainforests are dying,
E nergy is running out,
C an we make a difference?
Y es we can!
C limate change is speeding up,
L ook at the melting ice caps.
I hope we can all do our bit,
N ot say, 'Someone else can do it.'
G et everyone to recycle - it's great!

Richard Winrow (10)
St Richard's Catholic Primary School, Skelmersdale

Litter

Litter picker,
Leaf sweeper,
Keep the rubbish
In the bin.
Don't give up because you can do it.
So keep it nice and tidy.
If you keep it up
Your world will be a cleaner place,
So do it every day!

Francesca Riley (9)
St Richard's Catholic Primary School, Skelmersdale

To Make The World A Better Place

To make the world a better place,
We must get rid of all the hate,
There is no need to shout and fight,
It only makes an ugly sight,
Some people in the world have plenty,
So share with those whose plates are empty,
Everyone should get together,
Be friends and live in peace forever.

Joshua Brady (10)
St Richard's Catholic Primary School, Skelmersdale

Litter Picker

Litter picker
Recycle doer
Lolly licker
Clean the sewer
Planet saver
Material recycler
What am I?
Eco-monster.

Mia Jakeman (9)
St Richard's Catholic Primary School, Skelmersdale

Recycling

Right!
Every bottle, can or plastic counts!
Clean your environment!
You learn a lot about recycling!
Clever people recycle!
Learn that recycling is cool!

Megan Berry (10)
St Richard's Catholic Primary School, Skelmersdale

Clean Machine

Litter picker,
Lolly licker,
Put the wrapper in the bin,
Then you'll have a smiley grin.
I am kind called Clean Machine,
Not mean to the planet,
So what am I?
Eco-kid.

Jodie Chong (9)
St Richard's Catholic Primary School, Skelmersdale

Think Green

Think green, keep the world clean,
Put plastic in bins and recycle tins,
Turn off your light, we don't need it so bright.
Paper can be reused to save our trees,
Shoes can be sent to all in need.
Leave your car in the drive,
It cuts down pollution and prolongs your lives.
Think green, think green, think green.

Edward Vella (10)
St Richard's Catholic Primary School, Skelmersdale

Litter Picker

Litter picker
Planet lifter
Put the tin
In the bin
Help the planet
With a grin.

Megan Burns (10)
St Richard's Catholic Primary School, Skelmersdale

Eco·Kid

I'm a land saver
A planet craver
A flower planter
Weed killer
Don't waste paper
Don't be a traitor
Don't cut trees down
Or I'll have a frown.

Claire Walsh (9)
St Richard's Catholic Primary School, Skelmersdale

The Green Thing To Do

The horrible litter
Will be gone in a flicker
If you follow my rules.
So just follow the rules
Of St Richard's school,
Then the litter will be gone in a flicker.
Love food, don't start wasting,
Do the right thing, do the green thing.

Alex Kennedy (9)
St Richard's Catholic Primary School, Skelmersdale

Why Litter?

L iving
I n
T his
T errible
E xtraordinary
R efuse.

Sophia Sanchez-Sall (10)
St Richard's Catholic Primary School, Skelmersdale

Litter Picker

Litter picker, say no to litter
Saving the environment is saving the world.
The world will be a happier place.
Every minute, every place.
Every hour and every day.
Everyone is saving the environment,
Why not join us?

Jamie Wooding (9)
St Richard's Catholic Primary School, Skelmersdale

The Precious World

The world is precious,
Every bit
Please don't make a mess of it
Why destroy the sea?
It is bad for the animals and me.
Why destroy the sand?
It can make a beautiful land.

Abbi Dimmock (9)
St Richard's Catholic Primary School, Skelmersdale

Litter

Litter, litter, everywhere,
In the air and on the ground,
Litter, litter all around, up and down, it's everywhere.
Use a bin, they are for the rubbish,
Make the world a better place.

Aaron Usher (11)
St Richard's Catholic Primary School, Skelmersdale

Recycling

You can't just throw your rubbish away
It's not the right thing to do.

Think about the future
What a mess we're in.

Sort out your rubbish properly
Put it in the right coloured bins.

Recycle all away your metal, bottles
And all your food tins.

Recycle glass, paper and toys
You will help poor girls and boys.

Are you going to
Recycle?

Naeem Dawood (9)
Sharples CP School, Bolton

Why Not Peace?

Can't you see, starvation and war means dying?
There's nothing to love, nothing to watch, but pain and sorrow
Flooding the world.
People made to walk over bombs, as family get shot or forced
to join the army.
Long ago there was peace, each one of us was equal.
Some people want too much, they don't understand we are unique.
Fighting because you're made to, and fighting for how you are,
Pain and agony was born.
So why war, war?
Don't you think we're better off with peace?
When love is shared among those where hatred still remains,
More love is born.

Sufia Ruhomaun (10)
Tregoze Primary School, Swindon

Why War?

War is everywhere
In towns, in cities,
But nobody seems to care
Sadly people pass away
Taking memories of bombs falling
But why fight everyday?
What do you earn?
Power, happiness?
Or a dreadful turn?
So help stop war
Help to stop death
Save people for evermore
Our world is not happy
Children have been evacuated,
Country children think them tatty
So let them come back
Create more love
That is what we lack
Save war,
Save our world
Save peace from war for evermore.

Shona O'Dwyer (10)
Tregoze Primary School, Swindon

The World

The world is a beautiful place,
But people still don't have homes,
Throughout the years there are a lot of fears like wars, pollution too,
But bad things are happening, like animals dying because of us,
Smoking is bad because it is death,
So no more smoking, no more animal killing,
Give money to the poor
Just save the *world!*

Akash Rajendrakumar (10)
Tregoze Primary School, Swindon

War

Death is here and there is Iraq and across the world,
Where's the peace?
Where's harmony?
Why does it have to end in death?
What is the reward?
Land, power and anything else,
What do they want with innocent people?
They only do what they are told to
So hold the bombs
Don't fight, please.
The evacuees will be missing their mums,
They want to come home
But if there's no peace or home to go to, they can't,
The little girls and boys want to be back, not in the country
So stop war,
Now!

Susannah Moore (11)
Tregoze Primary School, Swindon

Litter

Animal extinction for coats and bags,
People should stop killing animals for fashion and rags.

Homeless people, nothing to eat,
Homeless people, nowhere to sleep.
Avoid pollution, disease, extinction
And litter, all by recycling,
The more the better.

Jake Tyson (10)
Tregoze Primary School, Swindon

Climate Change

Unplug your mobile phones
Switch off your TV

Save energy
Save the planet
Save the universe

Care about the future
Care about the world

The ice is all melting
Just like Ice Age the movie
The floods will come

Care about the future
Care about the world

Climate change
Climate change.

Jack Sewell (7)
West Walker Primary School, Newcastle Upon Tyne

Save The World Poem

S top wasting energy
A void killing the world
V ery harmful gases are killing the world
E veryone help today

T he ozone layer is getting thinner
H elp save the world today
E veryone's putting chemicals into the air

W ater levels are too high
O thers are suffering because of us
R un, walk and cycle instead of using cars
L eaders are trying to help
D on't destroy the rainforest.

Jack Lockhart (9)
West Walker Primary School, Newcastle Upon Tyne

Let's Be Green

Life is a cycle,
So let's recycle.

I am very keen,
I want to be green.

We need a solution,
To sort out this pollution.

It's not a hike,
To use a bike.

Use your soul
To make the Earth whole.

We need to stop
Before it gets on top.

Ryan Walsh (10)
West Walker Primary School, Newcastle Upon Tyne

The Sunshine Shines Down

The sunshine shines down on us every day,
It shines down on us when the children play,
But the Earth is getting too hot,
If it gets too hot all the trees will rot,
If you help this will stop,
Reduce your power in the shop,
So take care of nature and trees,
There's creatures disappearing, like the bees.
The water is rising too much,
It could all stop at your touch,
We all think the world's pretty like a flower,
But it's not going to be, if we keep using power,
So stop using gas and oil,
Treat the world like a friend, being loyal.

Chenise Long (9)
West Walker Primary School, Newcastle Upon Tyne

Homeless People

You need a home to keep you warm,
In the cold and wintry nights.
But no home to live in with no food or drink
Really cannot be right.
You quiver and shiver all day and night,
Feeling all alone in your cardboard home.
We need to help those people who are homeless,
And help them with all our might.
To give a little money to charity will do a lot of good,
Helping others less fortunate than us.
Could provide them with some food.
We have a very warm house, no shiver or quiver,
Those in need of shelter and warmth
It's what they should have.

Libi Spence (7)
West Walker Primary School, Newcastle Upon Tyne

Tidy Up

Litter, litter everywhere
Blowing in my face and hair
Makes me bitter to see lots of litter
Bins, bins everywhere
I see them here and there
It's not a sin to use a bin
It could make you grin
Mess, mess everywhere
Causes stress to those that care
Let's make a quest
To make less and less.

Elise Walsh (7)
West Walker Primary School, Newcastle Upon Tyne

Recycle

Recycle, recycle we all need to do
Newspapers, cardboard and plastic too.
Recycle your rubbish every day
Put it in the recycling bin, don't just throw it away.
Wash out bottles, cartons and tins
And together we can make a difference
And fill up our bins!
The bin men will come and take them away
So that they can be recycled and used another day.

Mark Spearman (8)
West Walker Primary School, Newcastle Upon Tyne

All About Life

There is litter in our streets.
In our gardens beneath our feet.
Animals eating poorly, and diseased too.
Other countries are at war!
Bombs going off a blazing war,
Houses falling down so fast.
Today In 2008 we have new big recycling bins,
We clean our waste and our tins
For our new recycling.

Korey Yeoman (9)
West Walker Primary School, Newcastle Upon Tyne

Pollution

Pollution, pollution
Is not God's work.
Pollution, pollution,
Is bad for the Earth.
Litter, litter is bad for one street.
Litter, litter, is not very neat.
Green, green is what we all need.
Green, green is the way to succeed.

Jordan Wood (8)
West Walker Primary School, Newcastle Upon Tyne

Don't Drop Litter

Litter kills animals
Litter pollutes seas
It kills fish and doesn't look good.
Be nice to our planet
Be nice to our homes.
Be nice to the animals,
And keep the world clean
Don't drop litter!

Shannon Taylor-Thorn (8)
West Walker Primary School, Newcastle Upon Tyne

The Litter Rule

Litter is bad, it makes me mad.
Litter is cool, when you use the rule.
When you don't use the rule it's cruel.
Be cool, put in the bin
The world will win
And make it a better place to live in.

Callum Tait (10)
West Walker Primary School, Newcastle Upon Tyne

The World's Future

Climate change is getting worse due to pollution.
But there's a way to stop it by reducing our carbon footprint.
To do so we can start recycling,
Stop littering,
Stop cutting down rainforests
And walk and cycle as much as we can.

The world's future is in our hands.

Caro Kanyange (8)
West Walker Primary School, Newcastle Upon Tyne

Litterbug

I am not a litterbug but some people are.
They drop litter wherever they go.
If everybody dropped litter you would not see the ground
So why do people drop litter when they can recycle the litter?
That will help the environment
And by helping the environment
You are helping people all over the world.

Chantelle Dixon (8)
West Walker Primary School, Newcastle Upon Tyne

Litter

L itter is a really bad thing, it damages animals
I n the sea, there are lots of animals
T hat are suffering, so please do not litter, please!
T o animals we are a threat and we do not want that do we?
E veryone can try to not litter only if they put their mind to it.
R emind everyone not to litter please.

Chanel Shaw (10)
West Walker Primary School, Newcastle Upon Tyne

Recycle

R ecycle because we don't litter,
E arth needs us!
C arbon dioxide we breathe out,
Y ou need oxygen to help you live.
C ycle to school and back, it will help the world.
L ots of carbon dioxide can kill us!
E veryone should care about the world because people need to live.

Courtney Dunlop (10)
West Walker Primary School, Newcastle Upon Tyne

My Litter Poem

When you drop litter it makes me feel bitter
Our world is in a big disgrace
You don't have to be strong
It doesn't take long
To find a bin and pop it in
It's good for our world to recycle our rubbish.

Joshua Tait (8)
West Walker Primary School, Newcastle Upon Tyne

Litter

We all get bitter when we see litter
So don't be a fool, follow the rule
Find a bin and put it in
And if you see some more
Use the bin, don't let it go.

Louise Robinson (8)
West Walker Primary School, Newcastle Upon Tyne

Rubbish, Rubbish Everywhere

Rubbish, rubbish everywhere
Rubbish, rubbish everywhere
Do your bit and pick it up
Rubbish, rubbish everywhere
Put it in the bin, please, if you care.

Chantelle James (7)
West Walker Primary School, Newcastle Upon Tyne

Litter

One day I saw a person throwing litter on the floor
I said, 'Hey don't do that.'
He said, 'I do what I like, you don't frighten me.'
I said, 'Then I'll get the policemen to arrest you,
It is against the law.'

Georgia Louise Pirnie (9)
West Walker Primary School, Newcastle Upon Tyne

Save Our Planet!

Don't drop litter
Then our world will glitter.
Save the trees,
And we will see the autumn leaves.
Don't go in the car,
Walk but you might not get far.
But who cares about it,
Would you rather walk and get fit?
And think of saving money!
If you ran out of it, it wouldn't be funny.
Think of global warming
Then we won't get the warning!

Jack Corfield (10)
Wimboldsley Primary School, Middlewich

Don't Drop Litter

Litter is bad, it's had its chance
So take a good glance
And see the sea it's full of litter
And lots of other little critters.
What's worst of all it falls on the ground
It gets stuck to your feet
Chewing gum is not nice to see.
Can you find the key?
Unleash the good and pull off your hood
See the bad, and try and save our country
If you have a wrapper and you chuck it on the floor
You think it doesn't matter.
But it does.

Caroline McAlinden (9)
Wimboldsley Primary School, Middlewich

Go Green

R ecycling will help climate change, so it is not always a pain
E arth is really good, but recycling will help it keep its wood
C hucking paper away is not good, put it in a recycling box then
  You'll feel good!
Y ou could recycle, that means your mum will buy you a new bicycle
  Made out of recycled material
C limate change is getting worse, if you recycle you won't have
  A curse
L itter is a big problem put it in a recycling box and that will make
  You as clever as a fox
I ce Age is getting worse, if we recycle we won't have a curse
N otice that it rains every day, if we recycle it can be sunny again
G o green and recycle you can still make a difference.

Jamie Donnelly (9)
Wimboldsley Primary School, Middlewich

Save Our Creatures

Animals are dying, it's not fair,
They deserve a life but no one seems to care
All kinds of wildlife are getting trapped in litter
It makes them think that humans are bitter,
People should know that we can't take a chance,
All you needed to do is pick up your litter and let the animals dance,
The animals will grin,
If you put your litter in the bin,
So make it stop
And don't let the animal population drop.

Ella Ross (10)
Wimboldsley Primary School, Middlewich

Make Earth Last Longer

P eople are destroying our planet
O nly we can help
L itterbugs everywhere what can we do?
L ovely animals in despair
U psadaisy what should we do
T ell your parents, teachers and friends
   We are going round the bend
I only want to help!
O ut of your car, get your bike or you should walk
N o, put that litter in the bin, if you do the world will win.

Megan Kelly (10)
Wimboldsley Primary School, Middlewich

Save The Animals!

Animals, animals everywhere
Are calling out in despair.
Their homes are going quick and fast,
Soon they'll be something in the past.
The dodo bird has disappeared,
Help all the birds or they might clear
Save paper, then save the trees,
You might just help the chimpanzees.
If you save these animals soon
We could help them by tomorrow afternoon.

Heather Louise Whincup (10)
Wimboldsley Primary School, Middlewich

Love Our World

Why don't we switch the TV off at the plug?
Cos when we do we can give our planet a hug,
Switch off the light when you're not around
Cos when you do you might save a pound,
Walk to school, don't use the car,
Why don't you cycle and you'll go quite far,
Save the paper, save the trees
You might just help the chimpanzees
If you keep this paper recycling lark up
You might soon be drinking out of a recycled cup!

Alice Young (10)
Wimboldsley Primary School, Middlewich

Save Our World!

If you pick up litter, the world will sing for joy,
So help by telling people; every girl and boy,

Never ever smile when you drop a crisp packet,
You don't want me to come to your door and make a racket!

Have you ever seen a grey bin outside your house?
If you have, then use it, or you'll feel as small as a mouse,

So help by *not* dropping litter; you can do a lot,
If you ever see someone littering, tell them to *stop!*

Amelia Shackleton (10)
Wimboldsley Primary School, Middlewich

Save The World!

Don't cut down trees
Oh please, please, please,
Save the air,
Please be fair,
Think about what's out there,
Don't drop litter it's a horrible sight,
Animals may suffocate, *they really might!*
Keep on going, I know you'll make it,
Pleas trust me, I wouldn't fake it!

Annabel Cole (9)
Wimboldsley Primary School, Middlewich

Litter Isn't Nice

L itter, litter everywhere, please pick it up and put it there
I f you have a snack please put the wrapper in the bin and
   Remember you can also recycle tin!
T ick-tock, you're wasting your time, please pick your litter up
   There's a long line
T ell people to pick up their litter, if you do you will get much fitter
E nsure to put your litter in the bin, if you do you will win
R ubbish bins, rubbish bins aren't being used, if you put litter
   On the floor, I won't be amused.

Tabitha Copeland (9)
Wimboldsley Primary School, Middlewich

Be Green Not Grey

L itterbugs everywhere don't even smile
I wouldn't want you to do it again and throw away in a pile
T o do it properly you have to start again
T hough even you have to make some notes, so get out your
   Notepad and pen
E verybody is doing it right, so stop
R emember the things I say and you will be on top.

Joe Elson (9)
Wimboldsley Primary School, Middlewich

Litter Is Bad

L eaving litter everywhere, is not helping animals in despair
I ce Age is destroying our world, including the animals.
T rees are made for animals to live in, they're not just for paper
T ry and save money by riding to school, not using the car
E verybody help the environment from destruction
R ecycle will help save our world from digging holes to put rubbish in.

Madison Gill (10)
Wimboldsley Primary School, Middlewich

Litter

L itterbugs throwing litter on the floor
I nside your home there are bins, use them not the street
T he crisp packets and wrappers, if you see them on the floor
   Pick them up, keep your Earth clean
T he Earth needs your help, turn off the lights, save energy
E arth needs your help, horrible gas is in the air
R eally important to go with green energy.

Thomas Gregory (10)
Wimboldsley Primary School, Middlewich

Young Writers Information

We hope you have enjoyed reading this
book - and that you will continue to enjoy
it in the coming years.

If you like reading and writing poetry drop
us a line, or give us a call, and we'll send
you a free information pack.

Alternatively if you would like to order further
copies of this book or any of our other titles,
then please give us a call or log onto our
website at www.youngwriters.co.uk

Young Writers Information
Remus House
Coltsfoot Drive
Peterborough
PE2 9JX
(01733) 890066